SPIRIT
of America®

THE *North Carolina* COLONY

By Judy Alter

Content Adviser: Eric Gilg, Department of History, University of Massachusetts, Amherst, Massachusetts

The Child's World®
Chanhassen, Minnesota

8

THE *North Carolina* COLONY

Published in the United States of America by The Child's World®
PO Box 326 • Chanhassen, MN 55317-0326 • 800-599-READ • www.childsworld.com

Acknowledgments

The Child's World®: Mary Berendes, Publishing Director

Editorial Directions, Inc.: E. Russell Primm, Editorial Director; Melissa McDaniel, Line Editor; Elizabeth K. Martin, Assistant Editor; Olivia Nellums, Editorial Assistant; Susan Hindman, Copy Editor; Joanne Mattern, Proofreader; Kevin Cunningham, Peter Garnham, Ruthanne Swiatkowski, Fact Checkers; Tim Griffin/IndexServ, Indexer; Cian Loughlin O'Day, Photo Researcher; Linda S. Koutris, Photo Selector

Photo

Cover: North Wind Picture Archives; Bettmann/Corbis: 10, 12, 13, 15, 19, 20, 21, 25, 33; Corbis: 9 (David Muench), 35; Getty Images/Hulton Archive: 14, 22, 23, 28, 32, 34; Historical Picture Archive/Corbis: 16, 17; North Carolina State Archive: 27, 29; North Wind Picture Archives: 8, 18, 26, 31; Stock Montage: 11, 24.

Registration

Library of Congress Cataloging-in-Publication Data
Alter, Judy, 1938–
  The North Carolina Colony / by Judy Alter.
     p. cm.—(Our colonies)
"Spirit of America."
Includes bibliographical references (p.   ) and index.
Contents: North Carolina's Indians—The struggle for settlement—The North Carolina Colony—Defiance, war, and independence—Postwar problems and statehood—Time line—Glossary terms.
  ISBN 1-56766-665-5 (alk. paper)
  1. North Carolina—History—Colonial period, ca. 1600–1775—Juvenile literature. 2. North Carolina—History—1775–1865—Juvenile literature. [1. North Carolina—History—Colonial period, ca. 1600–1775. 2. North Carolina—History—1775-1865.] I. Title. II. Series.
  F257.A56 2003
  975.6'02—dc21   2003003773

12   24   35

Contents

Chapter ONE

North Carolina's First People

PEOPLE PROBABLY REACHED THE AREA THAT IS now North Carolina 10,000 years ago. These people traveled from place to place, following the animals that they hunted. Many of these animals no longer exist, such as the giant bison and the huge, elephant-like woolly mammoths and mastodons.

Over time, the climate warmed. Animals and plants became more plentiful. The people living in what is now North Carolina stopped moving so much. In the spring, they fished in the rivers and the ocean. In the summer, they gathered fruit and nuts on the flatlands away from the coast.

Native Americans in what is now North Carolina began to settle in small villages around 1500 B.C. By about A.D. 1500, when Europeans

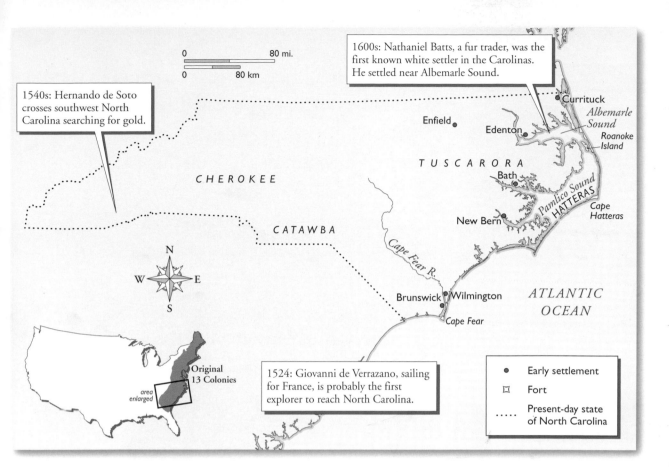

(map labels)

1600s: Nathaniel Batts, a fur trader, was the first known white settler in the Carolinas. He settled near Albemarle Sound.

1540s: Hernando de Soto crosses southwest North Carolina searching for gold.

0 80 mi.

0 80 km

Currituck

Albemarle Sound

Enfield

Edenton

Roanoke Island

TUSCARORA

Bath

Pamlico Sound

CHEROKEE

HATTERAS

Cape Hatteras

CATAWBA

New Bern

Cape Fear R.

N
W   E
S

Brunswick Wilmington

Cape Fear

ATLANTIC OCEAN

Original 13 Colonies

area enlarged

1524: Giovanni de Verrazano, sailing for France, is probably the first explorer to reach North Carolina.

• Early settlement

⌂ Fort

..... Present-day state of North Carolina

first arrived in North Carolina, about 30,000 Native Americans belonging to 30 different groups lived in North Carolina. The Cherokee people were one of the largest native groups in the region. They lived in the Appalachian Mountains. Other large groups included the Hatteras, the Catawba, and the Croatans. But the biggest group was the Tuscarora.

Native Americans in North Carolina farmed, growing corn, beans, and squash. They also grew tobacco. Men hunted animals such as rabbits and deer. They also built canoes,

North Carolina Colony at the time of first European settlement

Interesting Fact

▸ Native Americans began to farm and settle in villages between 1000 B.C. and 1500 A.D.

which they used for fishing. Their homes were made of wooden poles covered with the bark of trees. They lived in villages. Sometimes they protected their villages by building walls or digging ditches around them.

These groups were matriarchal. This means that family relationships were traced through the mother's family. Children often took the name of their mother's people. Children learned by watching their elders and listening to the stories they told. They were taught that each person's contribution to the community was important.

When the first European explorers arrived in what is now North Carolina, the Native Americans believed that the Great Spirit was testing them by sending strangers to their land. It was a difficult test. When the Europeans first arrived, they brought with them diseases that were new to the Americas, such as measles and smallpox. The native people had never before been exposed to these diseases, so their bodies could not fight them. Thousands of Native Ameri-

The Native American village of Pomelock was located in present-day North Carolina.

cans in North Carolina died from these diseases, and millions died across North America.

The native people also became angry as the Europeans took more and more of their land. By 1711, the Tuscarora were so angry that they attacked and killed many settlers. Many Native Americans were also killed, and their villages were burned. Finally, the Tuscarora were defeated, and many fled North Carolina.

Native American Art and Storytelling

ART AND STORYTELLING HAVE LONG BEEN VITAL TO THE CULTURE OF NATIVE Americans in North Carolina. Early Native Americans made designs on rocks, called petroglyphs. The largest petroglyph in North Carolina is Judaculla Rock. The petroglyphs on Judaculla Rock show hands, feet, a turtle, and a lizard. They were probably made between 3000 and 1000 B.C.

Storytelling was also important in Native American culture. The native people of North Carolina told their history in stories, since they had no written languages. A favorite Cherokee story had to do with how the storytellers learned some of their stories. In this story, animals and people once talked to each other often about their lives. But as years went by, people stopped listening to the animals and talked only among themselves. Finally, a young man was chosen to go live with the animals and again learn their languages. He then shared their stories with the people.

9

Chapter TWO

The Struggle for Settlement

Giovanni da Verrazano sailed along the North Carolina coast in 1524.

GIOVANNI DA VERRAZANO, AN ITALIAN working for the king of France, was probably the first European explorer to reach what is now North Carolina. In 1524, he sailed along the coast. Two years later, in 1526, a Spanish party of more than 500 men and women attempted to settle at the mouth of the Cape Fear River. Illness and starvation caused the settlement to fail. Then, in the 1540s, Spanish explorer Hernando de Soto crossed the southwest corner of what is now North Carolina while searching for gold.

Another group of Spaniards set out in 1566 to trade with the

Native Americans and convert them to Christianity. This group was headed for Chesapeake Bay, in what is now Maryland. But a storm blew them ashore in North Carolina. They claimed the land for Spain. Spain didn't think it was worth the trouble to keep it.

England also claimed the region. In 1584, England gave Sir Walter Raleigh a **charter** that allowed him to settle the land. Right away, Raleigh sent explorers to find a good place to build a settlement. They chose Roanoke Island. Raleigh's first colony was established in 1585. A man named Ralph Lane led 108 men to build Fort Raleigh. But the settlers did not have enough food, and they fought with the Native Americans. When a Native American stole a silver cup, the colonists burned an entire native village. A battle followed. In time, the colony failed and the colonists returned to England.

Sir Walter Raleigh was granted a charter that allowed him to settle the area that became North Carolina.

Interesting Fact

▶ Sir Walter Raleigh is considered the "Father of English America." He tried unsuccessfully to colonize North Carolina several times. He never set foot on colonial territory.

The baptism of Virginia Dare, the first baby born to English parents in America

In 1587, Raleigh sent 117 men, women, and children to Roanoke Island for a second try at founding a colony. On August 18, 1587, a baby named Virginia Dare was born on Roanoke Island. She was the first child born to English parents in America. A war between England and Spain kept English ships from returning to the colony until 1590. When ships finally arrived at Roanoke Island, there was no sign of the colonists. The only clue was the word "Croatan," the name of a local tribe, which was carved into a tree. No one knows what happened to the colonists. They may have starved to death. Native Americans may have killed them. Or they may have joined a

Native American tribe. Today, the settlement is known as the Lost Colony. Sir Walter Raleigh never succeeded in establishing a colony in the region.

It was many years before the English again tried to settle in the region. In 1629, King Charles I of England gave the land to Sir Robert Heath. The region was then called Carolina (the Land of Charles). But Heath did not settle the land, and it changed owners several times.

No one knows the exact date of North Carolina's first permanent European settlement. North Carolina calls itself a "state without a birthday." The first known white settler was a fur trader named Nathaniel Batts. He settled near Albermarle Sound, in northeastern North Carolina. By the 1660s, the colony of Virginia recognized that more people were moving to the region to the south. A sheriff was appointed to collect taxes and keep order. This was the beginning of North Carolina's government.

In 1629, King Charles I (above) gave the region known as Carolina to Sir Robert Heath.

THE 1700S WERE THE HEYDAY OF pirates on the southeastern coast of the United States. Pirates disrupted shipping and caused economic hardship for the people of Carolina. But people did not always mind pirates. They learned that pirates often sold supplies at a lower price than honest merchants.

The most famous pirate was Edward Teach, who was known as Blackbeard. The name Blackbeard came about because he put matches in his hat during a battle so that his head would always be surrounded by smoke.

The North Carolina coastline has many hidden waterways, inlets, coves, and creeks. It was filled with good hiding spots for Blackbeard. He often seized ships to steal their cargoes. In May 1718, he **blockaded** Charleston Harbor until he got medical care for his crew.

After that, Teach appeared to give up piracy. In 1718, he was allowed to build a home in the city of Bath. Governor Charles Eden of Virginia **pardoned** him for his crimes. But then he returned to piracy. The British sent two ships to capture him. In a surprise raid at sea, Blackbeard was killed and his crew was captured. Piracy died down after Blackbeard's death.

Chapter THREE

The Carolina Colony

IN 1663, A NEW CHARTER OFFICIALLY ESTAB-
lished the colony of Carolina. In the charter,
King Charles II granted the land
to eight wealthy Englishmen. This
was his way of repaying the debt
he owed them. They were called
the Lords **Proprietors** of Carolina.

People already living in Carolina, most of whom had moved
south from Virginia, resented the
Lords Proprietors. The Proprietors
ruled from England. They hired
governors to live in Carolina. The
governors charged colonists high
rent. Many of the governors were
also dishonest and ineffective. They did not
work for the good of all the colonists or do

*King Charles II granted the
charter for the Carolina
colony to eight wealthy
Englishmen in 1663.*

much to keep order.

Slave labor was important to the economy of North Carolina. At first, workers on the large farms called **plantations** were indentured servants from

Many enslaved Africans worked on tobacco plantations in North Carolina.

England. These were men, women, and children who could not afford to pay their own way to the colonies. They "indentured" or sold themselves to ship captains. On reaching the colony, the captains sold the indentured servants to tobacco farmers. A man working on a tobacco plantation could pay off his ship passage in four to five years. Then he was a free man.

As plantations grew, the need for field labor increased. Colonists enslaved Native Americans and Africans. Most slaves worked in tobacco fields from sunup to sundown. Slaves were also used in the fishing trade in North Carolina.

Many food crops, such as the rice grown on this plantation, were produced in colonial North Carolina.

Tobacco was the most important crop in North Carolina. Other important crops included corn, peas, beans, wheat, and rice. North Carolina produced so much food that it became known as the breadbasket of the colonies.

When some farmers began illegally trading tobacco with Scotland, the governor tried to collect taxes. In 1677, the farmers rebelled, jailed the governor, and ran the colony for two years. This became known as Culpeper's Rebellion.

In 1712, the proprietors divided the territory into North Carolina and South Carolina. In 1729, the king bought the colony from the proprietors. North Carolina became a royal colony, governed directly from Great Britain. This gave the region a more dependable government. Now the king would appoint the governor.

Only about 3,000 English people lived in the northern part of Carolina in 1689. But after becoming a royal colony, North Carolina grew rapidly. By 1775, it was the fourth-largest colony. People moved to North Carolina from other colonies and from Scotland, Wales, England, Germany, Ireland, and other countries. Most were escaping economic hardship.

Throughout the 18th century, Great Britain and France had been competing for the rich farmland and fur trade in the Ohio River valley, far to the west of North Carolina. In 1754, this competition turned into the French and Indian War. In the end, England gained all the land east of the Mississippi River. Though the French and Indian War was not fought in North Carolina, it would affect the colony. To pay for the war, Britain began imposing taxes on the colonies.

Interesting Fact

▸ The only good thing the Lords Proprietors did was to divide the Carolinas into North and South Carolina.

Though none of the battles of the French and Indian War were fought in North Carolina, the conflict still had an effect on the colony.

These taxes angered the colonists, since they had no representatives in the British government. The 1765 Stamp Act required that all printed material, including legal documents, newspapers, and even playing cards, have a stamp on them. The colonists had to pay for the stamps. They were a tax.

The Stamp Act aroused violent protests in North Carolina. North Carolinians protested in the cities of Wilmington, New Bern, and Cross Creek. Protesters kept a ship carrying stamps from docking at Brunswick. An armed group confronted Governor William Tryon, demanding that he not use the stamps. He gave in.

In 1768, a group from the western part of North Carolina, calling themselves the Regulators, withheld taxes and staged

The Stamp Act required stamps, such as these, to be attached to all printed materials sold in the American colonies. The colonists rebelled against having to pay for these stamps.

protests. They were particularly angry about the treatment of the poor and about how much money had been spent on the governor's home. They called it Tryon's Palace. The Regulators met Tryon's soldiers in the Battle of Alamance and were defeated. Some say the battle was the beginning of American rebellion against Britain.

A Women's Protest

WOMEN IN NORTH Carolina were not expected to be involved in politics. They were to keep house, prepare meals, make clothing, and raise children. But in Edenton, in about 1760, 50 women met to protest the fact that men in the colony could not vote in British elections. The women agreed not to buy English tea or clothes. This important protest was the first political act by colonial women against the British government.

Chapter FOUR

War and Independence

The First Continental Congress was held at Carpenter's Hall in Philadelphia, Pennsylvania, in 1774.

WHEN REVOLUTION CAME, MANY COLONISTS found it hard to give up their loyalty to Great Britain. Those who supported the Revolution were called Patriots. Those who remained loyal to Britain were called Tories, or Loyalists. North Carolina was a divided land.

In 1774, representatives from the colonies gathered in Philadelphia, Pennsylvania, for the First **Continental Congress.** They

JOURNAL

OF THE

PROCEEDINGS

OF THE

CONGRESS,

Held at PHILADELPHIA,

September 5, 1774.

PHILADELPHIA:

Printed by WILLIAM and THOMAS BRADFORD,
at the *London Coffee-House.*

DCC,LXXIV.

A printed copy of the journal that recorded the proceedings of the First Continental Congress

wanted to discuss their concerns over British rule. North Carolina governor Josiah Martin refused to allow the colony's **assembly** to meet and elect **delegates** to attend the

The Battle of King Mountain was one of the few Revolutionary War battles that was fought in North Carolina.

Continental Congress. So the people of North Carolina held the First Provincial Congress without the governor in 1774. This was the first elected assembly held in America in defiance of the British. North Carolina's Provincial Congress elected delegates to the Continental Congress.

In April 1776, the Fourth Provincial Congress met. It allowed North Carolina's delegates in the Continental Congress to join other colonies in declaring independence. This was the first official call for American independence in the colonies.

Few battles of the Revolutionary War were fought on North Carolina soil. Yet the state was deeply involved in the Revolution. It raised troops, equipped them, and maintained them. In 1780, the Patriots defeated British general Charles Cornwallis's troops at the Battle of King Mountain.

Charles Cornwallis was the commander of the British troops during the Revolutionary War.

▶ The Battle of
Guilford Court
House was one of
the bloodiest of the
Revolution. Colonial
casualties were 1,255,
but most turned out
to be missing, not
dead. The British
lost 93 men and
had 439 wounded.

American and British troops clashed in
North Carolina again the following March.
But American general Nathanael Greene was
not ready to confront Cornwallis's main
army. Greene's troops were defeated at the
Battle of Guilford Court House. But Cornwallis could not maintain his victory. He
surrendered to General George Washington
on October 19, 1781. The fighting in the
American Revolution was over. The new
nation was born.

*The Patriots lost the Battle
of Guilford Court House
to General Cornwallis
and his men.*

In 1775, British governor Josiah Martin fled North Carolina. The colony was ready to establish an independent government. The Fifth Provincial Congress met in 1776. In six weeks, delegates approved North Carolina's first constitution. This document gave the governor limited power. North Carolinians had had enough of governors with great power. The General Assembly that was created had more power. It chose all state executive officials and judges. The constitution was adopted December 18, 1776. Richard Caswell was chosen as governor. The General Assembly met for the first time in April 1777 in New Bern.

North Carolina's new government faced many problems. It had to recruit and train soldiers for the war. It had to deal with the turmoil in the western part of the state, where white settlers kept pushing the Cherokee off the land. It had to deal with Loyalists. And it had to unify the state and make the new constitution work.

Chapter FIVE

Problems after the War

The Revolutionary War came to an end when the British surrendered to General Washington at Yorktown, Virginia, in 1781 (below). Many North Carolinians fell into poverty after the war.

THE PERIOD AFTER THE WAR WAS DIFFICULT for North Carolina. The new state government was weak. Many North Carolinians fell into poverty. Both Patriot and Loyalist bands roamed the countryside, robbing and killing innocent people. This was called the Tory

War. David Fanning was the leader of the Tories. He killed women and children in his raids. When he fled to Canada in May 1782, the Tory War ended. But hard feelings remained in North Carolina. Many Loyalists left the state. At the same time, many Patriots who had been British prisoners of war returned home.

The government of North Carolina couldn't agree on where a new capital should be located. For many years, the assembly moved from town to town. Finally, land was bought to establish a new town as the capital. The new capital was named Raleigh.

The new United States of America also had difficulty establishing a government.

David Fanning, leader of the Tories, barely escaped to Canada.

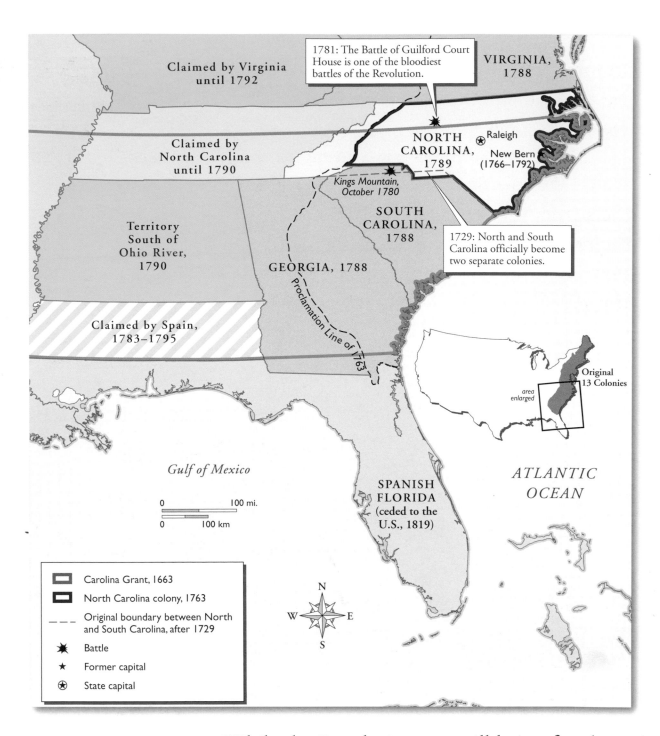

1781: The Battle of Guilford Court House is one of the bloodiest battles of the Revolution.

VIRGINIA, 1788

Claimed by Virginia until 1792

Claimed by North Carolina until 1790

NORTH CAROLINA, 1789

⊛ Raleigh

New Bern (1766–1792)

Territory South of Ohio River, 1790

Kings Mountain, October 1780

SOUTH CAROLINA, 1788

1729: North and South Carolina officially become two separate colonies.

GEORGIA, 1788

Claimed by Spain, 1783–1795

Proclamation Line of 1763

Original 13 Colonies

area enlarged

Gulf of Mexico

0   100 mi.
0   100 km

SPANISH FLORIDA (ceded to the U.S., 1819)

ATLANTIC OCEAN

▭ Carolina Grant, 1663

▭ North Carolina colony, 1763

– – – Original boundary between North and South Carolina, after 1729

✸ Battle

★ Former capital

⊛ State capital

N
W ✦ E
S

North Carolina Colony before statehood

While the Revolution was still being fought, representatives from the states put together a government based on the **Articles of**

Confederation. Under this document, the United States lacked a strong central government. It did not even have the power to tax.

By 1787, it was clear that this government wasn't working. Representatives from the states gathered in Philadelphia to discuss the problems with the Articles of Confederation. They ended up writing a new **constitution.** The U.S. Constitution gave the central government the power to tax. It also created a federal court system.

Raleigh eventually became the capital of North Carolina.

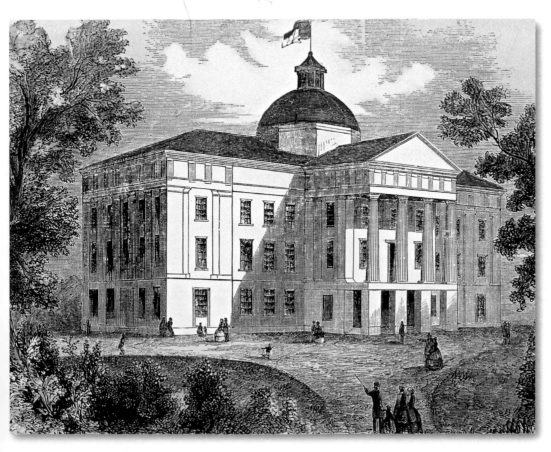

31

▶ North Carolina adopted its state flag in 1885. It has a white star in the center of a red field. The date Mary 20, 1775 is inscribed in a circular pattern. Below it is April 12, 1776, the date North Carolina resolved to join the other colonies in declaring independence.

Under the Articles of Confederation, the United States lacked a strong, central government.

A R T I C L E S

OF

CONFEDERATION AND PERPETUAL UNION,

BETWEEN THE COLONIES OF

NEW-HAMPSHIRE,
MASSACHUSETTS-BAY,
RHODE-ISLAND,
CONNECTICUT,
NEW-YORK,
NEW-JERSEY,
PENNSYLVANIA,

THE COUNTIES OF NEW-CASTLE,
KENT AND SUSSEX ON DELAWARE,
MARYLAND,
VIRGINIA,
NORTH-CAROLINA,
SOUTH-CAROLINA, AND
GEORGIA.

ART. I. THE Name of this Confederacy shall be "THE UNITED STATES OF AMERICA."

ART. II. The said Colonies unite themselves so as never to be divided by any Act whatever, and hereby severally enter into a firm League of Friendship with each other, for their common Defence, the Security of their Liberties, and their mutual and general Welfare, binding the said Colonies to assist one another against all Force offered to or attacks made upon them or any of them, on Account of Religion, Sovereignty, Trade, or any other Pretence whatever.

ART. III. Each Colony shall retain and enjoy as much of its present Laws, Rights and Customs, as it may think fit, and reserves to itself the sole and exclusive Regulation and Government of its internal police, in all matters that shall not interfere with the Articles of this Confederation.

ART. IV. No Colony or Colonies, without the Consent of the United States assembled, shall send any Embassy to or receive any Embassy from, or enter into any Treaty, Convention or Conference with the King or Kingdom of Great-Britain, or any foreign Prince or State; nor shall any Colony or Colonies, nor any Servant or Servants of the United States, or of any Colony or Colonies, accept of any Present, Emolument, Office, or Title of any Kind whatever, from the King or Kingdom of Great-Britain, or any foreign Prince or State; nor shall the United States assembled, or any Colony grant any Title of Nobility.

ART. V. No two or more Colonies shall enter into any Treaty, Confederation or Alliance whatever between them, without the previous and free Consent and Allowance.

Nine states had to approve the Constitution before it went into effect. Many North Carolinians were unsure about approving the new Constitution. They distrusted a strong central government. They wanted to protect the rights of individuals by keeping the central government weak. This was because they had suffered under strong rule by British governors.

Some of their concerns were answered when the Bill of Rights was added to the Constitution. This was a list of individual rights that are guaranteed, such as the right to free speech and freedom of religion. North

An illustration of the signing of the U.S. Constitution in 1787

Congress of the United States

begun and held at the City of New-York, on Wednesday the fourth of March, one thousand seven hundred and eighty nine.

[The engrossed Bill of Rights document, including the preamble and Articles the first through the twelfth, with signatures of Frederick Augustus Muhlenberg, Speaker of the House of Representatives; John Adams, Vice President of the United States and President of the Senate; John Beckley, Clerk of the House of Representatives; and Sam A. Otis, Secretary of the Senate.]

North Carolina led the states in the fight to get the Bill of Rights attached to the U.S. Constitution.

Carolina led the fight to attach the Bill of Rights to the Constitution. It is now the first 10 amendments, or changes, to the Constitution.

34

The Constitution went into effect on March 4, 1789. But North Carolina did not approve the Constitution until November 21, 1789. This means that North Carolinians did not take part in the first election under the Constitution, which was held on February 4, 1789. They had no representation in the first session of Congress, which began meeting in New York City on March 4, 1789. Still, North Carolina was part of a new nation, under a new government. And in the coming decades, the state would flourish.

No representatives from North Carolina were at Federal Hall (below) in New York for the first session of the U.S. Congress in 1789.

35

1500s   Cherokee, Tuscarora, Catawba, Hatteras, Croatan, and other native people live in what is now North Carolina.

1524   Italian Giovanni da Verrazano becomes the first European to sail along the Carolina coast.

1526   The Spanish attempt to settle at the mouth of the Cape Fear River, but the colony fails.

1585   Englishman Sir Walter Raleigh attempts to found a colony on Roanoke Island. The colony fails.

1587   Sir Walter Raleigh founds a second colony on Roanoke Island. Virginia Dare of the Roanoke colony is the first child born to English parents in America.

1590   English ships return to Roanoke Island, only to find that all the colonists have disappeared.

1663   King Charles II of England gives Carolina to eight men called the Lords Proprietors.

1712   Carolina is divided into North Carolina and South Carolina.

1718   The pirate Blackbeard is killed off the North Carolina coast.

1729   North Carolina becomes a royal colony.

1754   Britain begins fighting France in the French and Indian War.

1765   The British pass the Stamp Act, the first in a series of taxes on the colonists.

1768   A group of colonists in western North Carolina called the Regulators protest British taxes. They are defeated in the Battle of Alamance.

1774   The First Continental Congress meets to discuss their concerns over British rule.

1775   Fighting begins in the American Revolution.

1776   North Carolina becomes the first colony to vote for independence. The Declaration of Independence is approved.

1780   The Continental army defeats British troops in the Battle of King Mountain in North Carolina.

1781   British general Charles Cornwallis surrenders to George Washington, ending the fighting in the Revolution.

1782   Loyalists rob and kill people in the North Carolina countryside in what is known as the Tory War.

1789   North Carolina becomes the 12th state to approve the U.S. Constitution.

1794   Raleigh becomes the state capital of North Carolina.

Glossary TERMS

Articles of Confederation (AR-tik-uhls uv kon-FED-uh-ray-shun)
The Articles of Confederation was the first constitution for the United States. It was replaced by the U.S. Constitution in 1788.

assembly (uh-SEM-blee)
An assembly is a part of government that makes laws. North Carolina's First Provincial Congress was the first assembly held in the colonies in defiance of the British.

blockaded (blah-KADE-ed)
When a harbor is blockaded, it means that warships are preventing other ships from coming and going. In 1718, the pirate Blackbeard blockaded Charleston Harbor.

charter (CHAR-tuhr)
A charter is a document giving settlers permission to form a colony. Sir Walter Raleigh received a charter to found a colony in Carolina in 1584.

constitution (kon-stuh-TOO-shun)
A constitution is a document outlining the structure and basic laws of a government. North Carolina's first state constitution was approved in 1776.

Continental Congress (kon-tuh-NENT-uhl KON-griss)
The Continental Congress was a meeting of colonists that served as the American government around the time of the Revolution. Members of the Continental Congress approved the Declaration of Independence.

delegates (DEL-uh-guhts)
Delegates are people who represent other people at a meeting. North Carolina's First Provincial Congress elected the colony's delegates to the First Continental Congress.

pardoned (PAR-dund)
Pardoned means forgiving a crime without punishing it. Governor Charles Eden of Virginia pardoned the pirate Blackbeard for his crimes.

plantations (plan-TAY-shuns)
Plantations were large farms that grew a single important crop and usually used enslaved workers. Many North Carolina plantations grew tobacco.

proprietors (pruh-PRY-uh-tuhrs)
Proprietors were people given ownership of a colony. King Charles II gave Carolina to the Lords Proprietors in 1663.

William Blount (1749–1800)

Continental Congress delegate, 1782–83, 1786–87; Constitutional Convention delegate, 1787; U.S. Constitution signer; North Carolina senate general assembly member, 1788–90; southwest territory governor, 1790–96; Tennessee Constitutional Convention president, 1796; U.S. senator from Tennessee, 1796–97; Tennessee state senator, 1798–99

William Richardson Davie (1756–1820)

North Carolina legislature member, 1786–98; Constitutional Convention delegate, 1787; North Carolina governor, 1798–99

Cornelius Harnett (1723–1781)

Continental Congress delegate, 1777–79; Articles of Confederation signer

Joseph Hewes (1730–1779)

Continental Congress delegate, 1774–77, 1779; Declaration of Independence signer

William Hooper (1742–1790)

Continental Congress delegate, 1774–77; Declaration of Independence signer

Alexander Martin (1740?–1807)

Continental Congress delegate, 1786; Constitutional Convention delegate, 1787; North Carolina governor, 1782–85, 1789–92; U.S. senator, 1793–99

John Penn (1741?–1788)

Continental Congress delegate, 1775–78; Declaration of Independence signer; Articles of Confederation signer

Richard Dobbs Spaight (1758–1802)

Continental Congress delegate, 1783–85; Constitutional Convention delegate, 1787; U.S. Constitution signer; North Carolina governor, 1792–95; U.S. House of Representatives member, 1798–1801; North Carolina state senator, 1801–02

John Williams (1740–1804)

North Carolina house of representatives member, 1778–80; Articles of Confederation signer; North Carolina state senator, 1782, 1793–94. First cousin of John Williams of Montpelier, North Carolina (1731–1799), a delegate to Continental Congress, 1778–79, and justice of North Carolina state supreme court, 1779–99

Hugh Williamson (1735–1819)

Continental Congress delegate, 1782; Constitutional Convention delegate, 1787; U.S. Constitution signer; U.S. House of Representatives member, 1789–93

For Further INFORMATION

Web Sites

Visit our homepage for lots of links about the North Carolina colony:
http://www.childsworld.com/links.html

Note to Parents, Teachers, and Librarians:
We routinely verify our Web links to make sure they're safe,
active sites—so encourage your readers to check them out!

Books

Alex, Nan. *North Carolina.* Danbury, Conn.: Children's Press, 2001.

Bial, Raymond. *The Cherokee.* Tarrytown, N.Y.: Benchmark Books, 1999.

Shirley, David. *North Carolina.* Tarrytown, N.Y.: Benchmark Books, 2001.

Places to Visit or Contact

Historic Bathe
To tour North Carolina's first town
P.O. Box 148
Bath, NC 27808
919/923-3971

Oconaluftee Indian Village
To learn more about how the Cherokee lived in the 1700s and watch as
such objects as canoes and pottery are made the old way
P.O. Box 398
Cherokee, NC 28719
828/497-2315

Tryon Palace Historical Sites and Gardens
To see a reconstruction of the grand house where the British governor of
North Carolina lived
610 Pollock Street
New Bern, NC 28560
252/514-4900

Index

About the Author

JUDY ALTER, A NATIVE OF CHICAGO, ILLINOIS, NOW LIVES AND WRITES in Fort Worth, Texas. At night, Alter writes fiction and nonfiction for young readers. During the day, she is director of Texas Christian University Press. Alter's parents retired to Tryon, North Carolina, in 1969. She visited there often and grew to love the land, the climate, and the mountain crafts. Alter is the parent of four grown children and the grandmother of two girls. She has an Australian shepherd, Scooby, and a cat, Wynona.